I0532492

CENTERING DIVERSITY

A Guide for Understanding How
Diversity Shapes Our World

Tracie Daniels

PUBLICATION DATA

Creator:	Daniels, Tracie
Title:	Centering Diversity: A Guide for Understanding How Diversity Shapes Our World
ISBN:	979-8-9862661-0-7 (pbk.)
Notes:	Includes references.
Subjects:	Diversity Business Organizational Behavior Leadership Psychology, Industrial Adult Education
Publisher:	Synergy Consulting, LLC P.O. Box 451 La Plata, MD 20646

DISCLAIMER

DEDICATION

This book is dedicated to my husband, Charles. Thank you for being my sounding board, my confidant, my therapist, and my biggest fan. I also dedicate this book to my children, Cheyenne, Ricardo, and London, who bring out the best in me. I hope you're as proud of me as I am of you.

TABLE OF CONTENTS

INTRODUCTION

People write books for many reasons. Some have a passion they want to share with the world and find that a book is the best way to do that. Others have incredible imaginations that allow them to provide fantasy and fiction to many readers. I felt there was a great deal of confusion in understanding Diversity, equity and inclusion, and I wanted to provide a relatable way for people to connect to these ideas. I also was annoyed at some of the literature in the market around the concepts of Diversity, equity and inclusion and felt I needed to provide some real truth. This book was a journey for me to write and I hope it serves as a journey for you to read. I wanted to take the opportunity in this introduction to speak freely and openly about what I want the book to convey to readers and to have my intentions clear.

There are several books about Diversity, equity, and inclusion on the market and I did not want this to be yet another one of the same ole thing. I also wanted this book to be a counter-narrative to some books on the market suggesting that we should move beyond Diversity or that Diversity is not enough. Those books want to appeal to the mass of readers, particularly those who are tired of hearing about Diversity, never liked the idea of Diversity and want to move beyond Diversity. While I'm hoping my book will reach the masses, I do realize that it might not be received by some as well and I'm ok with that.

This is not another book about Diversity, equity, and inclusion. This book is about Diversity ALONE, more specifically, the power of Diversity. I want to talk about the very thing that many authors want to move away from because the conversation may be easier. It's easier to talk about inclusion and belonging because you don't have to talk about the need for differences, particularly racial/ethnic and gender differences. When you talk about belonging, you do not have to mention the fear associated with the dominant group somehow losing its power over time as the world becomes more and more diverse. When you talk about topics other than Diversity, you do not have to address the systems shaped by and for the dominant group to keep them in power. As a point of reference, when I refer to the dominant group, I'm describing any identity group in the majority of a population, be it gender, racial/ethnic, age, socioeconomic status, etc.

This book is about Diversity and my approach to helping people understand why Diversity is so critical and should be recentered is one I haven't seen other books address. My goal is to show the power, necessity, and true need for Diversity as a foundation for everything we know in our existence. From the representation of differences in nature, geography, and financial environments to how Diversity is the foundation for educational systems, and industries. I could have even explored the world beyond our planet and described how diverse the solar system is, with multiple planets distinctly different on purpose.

I'm hoping that as you read through the chapters, you'll gain an awareness and, more importantly, an appreciation for the power of Diversity and how we need it just as much as we need air. It is my goal to help you to develop a greater understanding of how Diversity has shaped the world in which we all exist and to somehow translate that understanding into an appreciation for why we should all embrace the Diversity of individuals as much as we have embraced the Diversity in other areas of life as we know it. When you stop to think about how we experience the world, it is mind-blowing to realize how fascinating life is because of Diversity.

CHAPTER 1

IT ALL STARTS WITH DIVERSITY

Since the evolution of the human species, there has always been a recognition and awareness of difference. The ancient Greeks believed there were four core elements from which everything in life evolved: earth, wind, fire and water. These elements are different and serve different purposes for maintaining life. Diversity is essential in sustaining life.

Diversity is defined as "the condition of having or being composed of differing elements". Composition and variety are also terms that come to mind to help better understand Diversity. Differing elements could include things, concepts, and individuals. Diversity exists on all levels and in all aspects of life. Recognizing Diversity in all forms is how we understand the world.

Diversity is the pillar of everything that drives society forward, including innovation. Think back to the great inventors in history. Their Diversity in race, background, experience, status, education, ethnicity, and culture inspired them to invent the very necessities used by everyone to support everyday living and being. Consider Garrett Augustus Morgan, Sr., an African American entrepreneur who invented the three-position traffic light or Guillermo González Camarena, a Latinx electrical engineer whose invention, the chromoscopic adapter, allowed people to watch television in color in the 1940s.

When we think about Diversity, most people think of race and ethnicity. And while race and ethnicity may be the most salient aspect of Diversity, there are so many ways difference is expressed and lived. Diversity reflects other dimensions of the human experience, including but not limited to gender identification and expression, age, sexual identity, religion, culture, and ability. Diversity defines our preferences, belief systems, social systems, and ultimately how we show up in the world. Diversity acts as the foundation for how society operates. It is the glue that holds communities together and allows for different cultures to thrive.

Diversity is essential for social progress. It is only through Diversity we can see the world from different perspectives and develop new ideas. When everyone thinks alike, society stagnates. Diversity encourages innovation and creativity. It helps us to solve problems in exciting and innovative ways.

Diversity is so integral to society that studies on it have emerged as a distinct academic discipline in recent years. The study of Diversity examines how people are different and how those differences are used to create social hierarchies. It also looks at how people can work together to overcome these hierarchies. Ultimately, Diversity is what makes our world so rich and vibrant. Our societies are built upon this foundation.

The term "Diversity" can be traced back to social and political movements in the 1960s. In the United States, the Civil Rights Act, which made discrimination based on race, color, sex, religion, or natural origin unlawful, informs how we view Diversity today. While Diversity has a distinct definition, some argue that without context, the word Diversity is meaningless.

Diversity as we know and use it today was officially coined in 1978 as part of the judgement given in University of California v. Bakke in which race was allowed as a factor in college admission policies.

The study of Diversity has grown exponentially since then. This spike may also be attributed to the expansion in examining different types of Diversity in society, including different age demographics and genders. Today, examining Diversity in the workforce through a lens that includes differences in race, gender, nationality and other factors are becoming more prevalent.

In today's workforce, Diversity is a topic that takes center stage, especially for large organizations. Unfortunately, although Diversity has been around for decades, many companies have failed to prioritize examining their workforces properly and effectively due to short-term financial benefits. To truly enhance the Diversity of our workforce — including race, age and gender differences — organizations must first identify the root cause of underrepresentation through comprehensive data collection.

Research has suggested that a diverse workforce often provides a competitive advantage for companies. A good example of this is the U.S Department of Agriculture (USDA), which has been increasing its Diversity initiatives while simultaneously improving organizational performance and developing new products that have the potential to save companies millions of dollars.

There is a growing appreciation of Diversity in all aspects of society. Businesses realize that they need a workforce that reflects the Diversity of their customers. Schools recognize the importance of teaching students at a very young age about the differences in our cultures and beliefs. And governments are recognizing the importance of promoting Diversity and inclusion. Yet, the progress for improving Diversity in these societal institutions is very slow and at times, stagnant.

According to the US government census performed in 2020, the racial Diversity index score will be 0.73, which reflects a Diversity index score of 73 percent. This simply means that the Diversity in America will have increased by 23 percent from 2010 levels. While Diversity is evident in all forms, Diversity on race and ethnicity is still necessary to foster a meaningful society.

While there has been significant growth in racial/ethnic Diversity in the United States, we still see a lack of racial/ethnic representation in key industries, such as technology and creative fields. According to a Diversity report issued by Google in 2014, Diversity in technology is lacking due to the Diversity of thought that can arise from individuals with different backgrounds and experiences. Organizations like Google share a responsibility to ensure that current and future strategies are designed to increase the number of racial/ethnic professionals in the technology sector.

Typically, Diversity is associated with inclusion, equity and most recently belonging. When we speak about this work, we capture it under the heading of DE&I. However, Diversity is the key that makes these other concepts possible. There is no equity or inclusion in homogeneity.

Diversity cannot take a back seat to other concepts such as equity, inclusion, or even belonging because without it, none of those concepts would be possible. Diversity needs to be prioritized on both macro and micro levels to allow for equity and inclusion strategies to be effective in societal transformations and resolutions.

For decades, this has been a conversation that has been had amongst minority groups. However, the 2020 murders of George Floyd, Breonna Taylor, Ahmaud Arbery, and countless others, the social justice protests influenced by the Black Lives Matter movement (as a revitalization of the Civil Rights Movement), and a catastrophic world health pandemic that disproportionately affected people of color brought Diversity to the forefront in the United States once again. Diversity is no longer just a "minority" issue, it is a national issue that requires true systemic change.

Until we have critical transformative conversations about dismantling the current power and authority structures that have fostered the ongoing oppression of minority groups, we will not experience true change. Unfortunately, those transformative conversations cannot happen without significant representation of racial/ethnic groups in positions of power and authority. Significant representation of racial/ethnic individuals in these positions may not be a number or percentage of the total group, but enough representation so there is no dominant group represented. Further, this representation of racial/ethnic individuals in positions of power needs to be applied to every societal institution such as, government, economic, education, health, job market and communities.

To understand how far the road is ahead towards the destination, it's important to identify how far you've travelled. To determine how close we are to significantly representing racial/ethnic individuals in positions of power, we need to understand the current state. To simplify this examination of the current state, we only need to point to all of the societal institutions in the United States and recognize that positions of power are overwhelmingly occupied by White Americans as the dominant group. We have a long road ahead in working to achieve significant racial/ethnic representation in positions of power. However, at the individual level, there are changes that can be made to promote Diversity, starting with acknowledging the importance of Diversity and making it a priority in our lives.

Let's break it down to something simple that everyone experiences every day. When preparing a meal, you have various foods, herbs, and spices that form part of the recipe. If you remove one ingredient, it can alter the taste or consistency of the dish and sometimes even ruin it completely. The point here is, that without all these different components, you will not achieve your expected outcome. Each component, while different, contributes to the successful taste of the meal.

Diversity is a spectrum. It's not a one size fits all solution. We cannot forget the importance of having a seat at the table for everyone, regardless of their background or identity. We all have something unique to bring to the conversation, and we need to make sure that everyone can share their voice. Representation matters. One group cannot speak for everyone or understand the unique experiences faced by other groups. Richard Delgado, a legal scholar and a founder of critical race theory, wrote a piece for the Michigan Law Review in 1989 on storytelling for oppositionists. He describes how stories of the oppressed should be narrated and told by members of the oppressed group and how society should allow those stories to be heard. He also points out the danger of the dominant group telling stories of the oppressed and changing the narrative.

"In civil rights, for example, many in the majority hold that any inequality

between blacks and whites is due either to cultural lag, or inadequate

enforcement of currently existing beneficial laws - both of which are

easily correctable. For many minority persons, the principal instrument

of their subordination is neither of these. Rather, it is the prevailing

mindset by means of which members of the dominant group

justify the world as it is, that is, with whites on top and browns and

blacks at the bottom."

"Members of the majority race should listen to stories, of all sorts,

in order to enrich their own reality. Reality is not fixed, not a given.

Rather, we construct it through conversations, through our lives together.

Racial and class-based isolation prevents the hearing of diverse stories and counter stories. It diminishes the conversation through which we create reality, construct our communal lives."

Diversity should be more than just a theoretical view, but a tangible outcome.

To experience meaningful change, organizations and institutions in our society need to abide by what I call the DRIVE Principle.

Diversity

Reveals

Initiative

Vision

Expectations

Organizations that embrace and include a significant representation of multicultural perspectives demonstrate strong initiative through solving complex problems, dismantling the status quo, leading the market in their field, and developing innovative solutions that others will adopt. Institutions that center Diversity as evidenced by the significant representation of racial/ethnic groups have a clear vision of their current state and future state. Finally, when Diversity is the foundation for any societal structure, expectations for all who operate in those structures are not only met, but often exceeded.

When the element of Diversity is defined as concepts and constructs, it acts as the foundation for the sustainability of multiple systems. Within financial markets, industries, geography, educational studies, and types of jobs, rich Diversity creates an abundance of opportunity and creativity for every person. However, when Diversity is defined as different "groups of individuals", it takes on an entirely new meaning met with resistance. What would happen if the understanding of Diversity when applied to concepts and constructs was translated to gain a broader understanding of Diversity when applied to individuals?

CHAPTER 2

DIVERSITY IN FINANCIAL MARKETS

It is widely known that the key to successful financial investing is to diversify your holdings. The history of the financial market dates back centuries, with different types of investments and trading strategies emerging over time. The first stock market is believed to have originated in Amsterdam in the early 1600s, with merchants trading shares of companies. In subsequent years, other stock markets emerged in Philadelphia, London, New York, Paris and more. This expansion of the stock market indicates the need for Diversity in how cities and countries demonstrate economic growth.

Until the 1800s, or even later, entry to most stock markets was restricted to wealthy people with a large stake in a particular company. This meant that many people could not afford to buy shares of stocks and therefore did not have access to information about how companies were performing. The London Stock Exchange remained exclusive until after World War II, when eventually membership was left open to anyone with a trading account, whether or not they were an individual or a corporation.

Over time, new types of securities emerged on exchanges around the world. Besides stocks and bonds, options contracts and many types of derivatives became common. Exchanges traded in commodities and currencies. This development of different products proved critical to the advancement of the economy. It's clear that providing different streams of investment options lead to better overall economic performance. Diversity within the stock market was necessary for the economy to survive. Countries also developed their own stock markets so companies within a country could raise funds to support only that specific country. This allowed for more cultivation of diverse products within a country.

Diversity is a key part of our global capital markets today. The history of fixed-income investments dates back thousands of years with evidence suggesting that at least 3,000 years ago, people were exchanging formalized debt agreements. Diversity has shaped the fixed-income landscape by introducing new asset classes to the market. A fixed income asset can be broadly defined as a fixed-term investment that generates payments at regular intervals. Fixed-income assets are cheaper to purchase than other assets, making them generally less volatile, providing more stable payments.

Fixed-income assets are typically bonds for local, state, or federal governments. But are not confined to just these assets. Other assets are typically assets of stocks, certificates of deposit, or savings bonds.

The origins of securities trading can be traced back to ancient China when businessmen made transactions on goods or commodities through promissory notes or bonds known as "jiaozi". These notes were issued by merchants instead of payment in cash. It was not until later, during the Song Dynasty, that short-term negotiable certificates of deposit were introduced that can be considered as the earliest form of capital market financing instruments. Different securities have been known to many civilizations throughout time, including ancient Greece and Rome.

The origin of modern financial markets dates to medieval Europe, where trading in high-risk debt began with the prototype stock exchanges emerging in Italy in 16th century Venice and Genoa. By 1793, London's Stock Exchange had over a hundred members. The Industrial Revolution laid the foundations for relatively large production units producing goods such as iron, steel and coal, which resulted in concentrated industrial mass production not seen before this period. This era also saw new financial innovations being developed, such as the first derivative contracts - futures contracts on commodities. The railroad boom in the United States during the 1800s saw a dramatic expansion in capital markets as entrepreneurs issued stocks and bonds to finance their ventures.

The 20th century was a period of enormous transformation with two world wars and multiple economic depressions. Along with these events were important regulatory developments such as the Securities Exchange Act in 1934, which regulated the securities industry and aimed to protect investors by requiring listed companies to disclose material information. In addition, new financial products were created, including mutual funds, investment trusts, and pension funds. With each experience with stagnant investment products, it was necessary to add new products to provide more sustainability in the market. Diversity, once again, was the answer to stagnation.

Developing new investment vehicles and trading strategies has been central to the growth of the financial markets. For example, in the late 1800s, railroad companies issued bonds to finance their expansion. This helped to create a new type of investment known as a bond.

There has been an increase in Initial Public Offerings (IPOs) as companies go public in recent years, this can largely be attributed to Diversity. According to a study by Goldman Sachs, companies with female board members have a better chance of going public than companies that have no women on their board. The study also concluded that companies with women on the board are more likely to raise capital through IPO than companies without women in leadership positions.

Diversity on the board is important for a number of reasons. A diverse board can better identify and capitalize on new opportunities and challenges within the company, but most importantly, eliminate bias. It also makes for a more well-rounded board, which could be a more attractive prospect to investors.

The economy requires a certain amount of Diversity to ensure that it is prosperous. A lack of Diversity in an economy means that one or a few industries dominate the economy. Typically, these are highly susceptible to external shocks that can destabilize the economy. For example, if most of the economy is based on oil production, reducing oil prices will cause the economy to contract. Financial Diversity ensures that the economy is more resilient to external shocks and thus is more sustainable.

Financial Diversity is needed to create a thriving, sustainable and prosperous economy. Financial Diversity is the concept that the best economic success comes from mixing different sectors of the economy. The most common example of this is the strategy employed by venture capitalists. A venture capitalist provides capital for a business startup. The term "venture capital" was coined in the mid-20th century by Georges Doriot to describe financing for newly emerging, often high-risk business ventures. While venture capitalists do not provide equity for established companies, the term is often used colloquially to refer to firms providing such financing to startups, particularly technology and life sciences companies. These are typically private, for-profit firms that invest in new and developing businesses.

They invest in a variety of sectors, from low-risk, low-reward assets to highly experimental, high-reward assets. They do this because they know that if they just invest in one sector, they set themselves up to fail. The same applies to economies.

The United States of America was supposedly founded with the goal of equality among all its people. However, equality has never been obtained, despite mediocre efforts. Our financial system as we know it was originally established to support the wealthy and not too much has changed today. The institution of slavery in the United States led to a significant divide in how the country viewed wealth, more specifically, those who can obtain it. Ownership of property defined the wealthy class. It separated the haves from the have-nots. Because slaves were viewed as property and not individuals, wealth attainment for slaves was non-existent. However, the labor from slaves made many White men wealthy.

After the emancipation of the slaves around 1865, it was still next to impossible for former slaves to work, let alone obtain wealth. During the period of Reconstruction 1865 – 1877, a select few of Black men served in public office. However, those opportunities were cut short when reconstruction ended and implementation of Jim Crow separate, but equal laws were enforced.

It is no surprise that historically, only certain people could invest in stock markets. However, this has changed over time, and online trading has allowed anyone to invest in the stock market. In the mid-1900s, individuals who had the right to vote were the only ones allowed to invest.

The benefits of everyone investing are numerous, including higher participation rates and broader ownership. Research has shown that greater Diversity in the owner base of publicly traded companies is associated with better operating performance. And the benefits of broadened ownership have been demonstrated in the United States' Employee Stock Ownership Plan (ESOP) movement. Employee ownership provides a viable and stable alternative to the traditional pension for middle-income earners and has the potential to increase retirement savings for all Americans.

The stability of a country's financial Diversity is a key factor in determining whether its economy will be sustainable. It is also a key factor in determining whether a nation will be prosperous. A country too dependent on any one sector of its economy is vulnerable to collapse if that sector is lost.

Investments are a crucial part of every financial plan. This is because your investments can help you meet your financial goals. However, not all investments are equal.

A portfolio is a selection of financial instruments such as stocks, bonds, and other types of assets, owned by a single investor or a group of investors. The objective of a portfolio is to maximize returns with a limited amount of risk. Investors can choose from many types of portfolios, but there are two primary categories: active and passive. An active portfolio manager manages the holdings of a portfolio to meet specified investment goals. A passive portfolio manager typically tracks a market index, such as a stock market index, and attempts to match its performance.

As a general rule, Diversity is a good thing for investors. It reduces risk through a variety of asset classes, industries, and factors. A diversified portfolio is harder to beat. In the investment world, this is often expressed as "Don't put all your eggs in one basket."

Diversity in the investment portfolio is defined as the variability of returns caused by the mixing of investments. Too much of the same item in a portfolio can lead to increased risk and lower returns. This can be explained by the 'law of large numbers'. This law states that the larger the sample size, the closer its average will be to the expected value. This is why diversification is important. It reduces the standard deviation of the portfolio.

Diversity in investment is a portfolio construction strategy that aims to reduce the risk of loss while maximizing return. Diversity in investments means that a portfolio is made up of different asset classes, such as stocks, bonds, and cash, which tend to perform differently under different market conditions. A diversified portfolio can help protect investors from losing substantial money due to the failure of a specific investment or economic sector. There are three main types of diversification:

1) Asset class diversification,

2) Market capitalization diversification, and

3) Industry diversification. Many asset classes are positively correlated with each other.

Meaning, when one goes up, another is likely to go up. However, certain asset classes typically move in the opposite direction. For example, the stock market generally goes up when the bond market goes down. This means they are negatively correlated. If you can find assets negatively correlated, you can create a portfolio with returns that are not dependent on the overall market.

There are many investment strategies based on diversified portfolios that yield the most sustainable returns. Some of these include:

- Growth Investing: Growth investing is the practice of buying stocks of companies that have shown strong growth over the last several years. Growth investors are typically interested in companies with fast-growing revenue and earnings.

- Value Investing: Value investing is the practice of buying stocks of companies that look cheap compared to their fundamental value. Value investors are typically interested in companies with a low price-to-earnings ratio.

- Dividend Investing: Dividend investing is the practice of buying stocks that pay dividends. Dividend investors are typically interested in stocks with a history of growing their dividend payments over time.

Diverse companies can withstand financial downturns because they can sell different products or services. In comparison, less diverse companies rely heavily on one type of product or service, which can be very risky. For example, Kodak was a giant in the world of photography and film for over a century. However, their failure to innovate through diversifying their product offerings led them to an avoidable demise. There are similar stories of companies, such as Borders Books and Music, Blockbuster, and Xerox, which kept a homogeneous focus and failed to explore and invite new perspectives and ideas. Diversity remains the key to the success and sustainability of the financial sector and business.

CHAPTER 3

DIVERSITY IN EDUCATION

The education system in the United States and worldwide comprises diverse subjects and areas of study. In examining K-12 and college (undergraduate and graduate) education programs, the subjects from which an individual can choose are vast. Further, the aptitude tests and college preparatory exams, such as the SAT assess an individual's exposure to various subjects. The Diversity of subjects and areas of study are critical to ensuring that individuals develop a wide range of knowledge to contribute to and sustain our society.

K-12 schooling in America can be traced back to the early colonists. Early American children received education at home, with boys learning about civics and moral values and girls receiving basic reading, writing, and arithmetic skills. During the colonial era, children from wealthier families were often sent to grammar schools near their homes, but education was not compulsory. As the settlement grew westward, one-room schoolhouses became a common sight as communities pooled their meager resources to bring education to their children.

After the Civil War, industrialization brought increased immigration to America's cities. Unable to keep up with the influx of students, many one-room schools closed or combined with others for economies of scale. To help address this problem, philanthropists, including Andrew Carnegie began donating money for school construction projects in the second half of the nineteenth century; so when the Progressive Era arrived, they already had a network of schools in place. By the end of the 19th century, roughly one-third of all tax revenue was allocated toward education.

The K-12 common curriculum of subjects represents centuries of progress in our education system, from elementary schooling to high school. Though it is constantly evolving, one of the main goals has always provided students with a greater sense of Diversity within their studies.

The Common Core State Standards, or the Common Core, is a set of standards designed to increase the overall consistency and quality of academic standards in schools throughout the nation. It was originally developed through participation by teachers, school administrators, parents, and other educators. The standards focus on a balanced curriculum of core academics, including English language arts, mathematics, science, and social studies. Developing these standards began in 2009 and has since seen support from both Republican and Democratic leaders and numerous educational organizations.

K-12 schooling in America is now a detailed assessment of academic standards, challenges and opportunities encompassed by public education in the United States. Key elements include current challenges and activities, outcomes-based curriculum design and specific skills development, and educational financing mechanisms and special opportunities attained by minority groups.

The purpose of the K-12 achievement tests provides information about the academic progress of students. The results are used by educators, parents, policymakers and the public as a gauge of student success, and a formative assessment tool to help teachers and schools identify strengths and weaknesses in their students' knowledge and skills.

A strong foundation in K-12 education begins with a well-rounded, balanced curriculum. While every student will have his or her own interests, it is important for students to have exposure to a diverse set of subjects. The more exposure a student has to different subjects, the more well-rounded he or she will become.

By studying a varied selection of topics and skills, children are more likely to continue their education with sufficient knowledge in a variety of areas - increasing their chances to succeed in college or on their own as adults.

After high school, there are an even larger variety of higher education options for students in the United States. From community colleges, technical or trade institutions, junior colleges, four-year colleges and universities all the way to professional training programs and postgraduate studies, many students can find various levels of education at a school that fits their needs. The power of Diversity is demonstrated through having multiple pathways to achieve.

The Diversity of the United States' educational system is truly unparalleled. The United States has over 5,000 colleges, universities and technical institutes—about 15 percent are public institutions. Across the country, there are over 850 public institutions that enroll 22 percent of college students; over 400,000 teachers at these schools educate about 12 million full-time students each year. These numbers barely scratch the surface of what makes up this country's educational Diversity—besides public and private institutions, there are also special institutions such as historically Black colleges and universities (HBCUs), Hispanic Serving Institutions (HSIs), and Tribal Colleges and Universities (TCUs).

HSIs are recognized in the United States and are public colleges and universities with a full-time undergraduate student enrollment of at least 25 percent Hispanic. There are over 500 HSIs in the United States.

TCUs have three basic criteria: they must be tribally chartered, their boards must comprise a majority of Native Americans, and the student body must comprise a majority (51 percent) of Native Americans. Many of the TCUs are on or near Native American reservations. These institutions provide unique access to quality educational opportunities for Native Americans while providing educational and social services to the tribal communities.

HBCUs were founded during the early 1800s to serve the Black community by providing quality education to students. The accessibility of quality educational programs at HBCUs provides equal opportunities for students to receive an education regardless of their socio-economic or cultural background. HBCUs not only focus on Diversity within the college environment but also on other academic experiences. HBCUs are dedicated to providing culturally focused curricula, creating academic programs that address social issues, and developing an atmosphere of communication among students and faculty. HBCUs promote strong relationships between students and faculty, thus creating individualized learning within a social environment due to building Diversity within their campus community.

The Diversity of college courses is needed to build a secure foundation for learning and achievement, which leads to a meaningful career, a functioning citizenry, and an engaged society. Further, a diverse educational·system cultivates more informed and educated individuals knowledgeable about various fields.

The benefits of a diverse college curriculum can be seen in its influence on job success, community development and civic engagement. With over 22 million students completing college degrees in the United States every year, the importance of Diversity within the collegiate experience should be heavily considered.

College students need a diverse curriculum. A well-rounded education is a mix of courses in the liberal arts and sciences, including courses that teach the benefits of Diversity, familiarity with the relativism of values, and the importance of religion and ethics.

Colleges like The University of Tulsa are a great example of Diversity as they boast 67 undergraduate programs, 47 graduate programs, and 10 doctoral programs. It is one of the nation's top universities, home to 6 colleges and schools ranging from business to engineering and from arts and sciences to medicine.

The core curriculum at The University of Tulsa offers a variety of courses designed to lay the foundation for their students' undergraduate experience. By taking courses from various disciplines, students gain an appreciation for many points of view and develop their own identity and set of skills. The courses in the core curriculum give students the breadth they need to become successful in the diverse workforce TU graduates enter.

The benefit of this diversification is that it allows more people to find a career that works for them. The economy flourishes because people can find the jobs they are passionate about. This ability to choose between different types of educational paths increases the productivity of the overall economy because the supply of workers is not concentrated in a few areas.

Diversity is a fundamental part of the learning experience on any college campus. This may be because diverse socio-economic backgrounds, cultural traditions, and experiences create a classroom dynamic that is more conducive to learning. In addition, students learn various ways of thinking from different perspectives that broaden their world views.

The traditional four-year degree is no longer the only option for students. With the rise of online education, trade schools, community colleges, technical schools, certificate programs, apprenticeships, students are no longer limited to four-year degrees or institutions. They can now take courses from any school without having to physically be there.

Online learning, for instance, has been around for a long time but it was never as accessible as it is today. This change has been driven by technological advancements in our society and the need for lifelong learning.

Many students are now choosing short-term programs that provide them with the skills to enter the workforce quickly. These programs allow students to work while they learn, which is perfect for those who want to work right away after high school.

Education is like a tapestry, composed of different threads. Each offers unique benefits, but they are all parts of the same whole. Students have diverse skills, personalities, and learning styles. In the same way that a student may take notes in different ways based on their style, different students may learn best from different sources. There are several channels that students can use to gain an education: physical textbooks, online textbooks and course materials, online libraries and databases, discussion boards and peer-reviewed journals or articles, and in-person sources such as teachers and peers.

Overall, Diversity in education is vital to a comprehensive and cohesive education and the development of innovative and creative ideas and solutions. If a student's studies are limited to their immediate areas of knowledge, such as math or computers, for example, their thoughts would be limited only to subjects that directly relate to these subjects. If a student were exposed to subjects outside of their normal field of study, they could apply this new knowledge in different ways. The power of Diversity within the educational system allows for a plethora of possibilities to shape an individual's intelligence.

CHAPTER 4

DIVERSITY IN GEOGRAPHY

There are many countries with different cultures, religions, and laws. In a globalized world, these differences have established a network of diverse societies that work together for their mutual benefit. This collaborative network is what the world actually needs to connect everyone and allow people to experience cultural Diversity.

Throughout the centuries, diverse cultures and societies have influenced each other. And today is no different. Today we live in a world where cross-cultural influences are more relevant than ever before. Experiencing this global society of difference is necessary for nations to continue to grow, innovate and survive. We all benefit from the different ideas, customs, products, and way of living that each society offers. Each culture, in its magnificent uniqueness works to contribute to one universal culture. Through trade and opportunity, anyone can experience the best that a particular country offers. For example, China is the leading manufacturer of cars. Countries, including the United States, Italy, France, Russia and South Korea, have enormous exporting power that allows other countries to benefit from the diverse products and services to build and sustain way of living. It would be ridiculous to think that one country can do it all. The reality is that we need each other, and we benefit from the unique contributions that other every country offers. Any culture, no matter where it exists in the world is shaped by the culture of others. That's the power that Diversity creates.

Throughout history, people have lived in all kinds of landscapes: small mountain villages to dense large cities. Our landscapes have been shaped by many factors like natural resources, weather patterns, economic circumstances, and political events. It is a fact that our geographical landscape is inherently diverse. Different climates, topography, and environments define the flora and fauna, which determine the food which ultimately influences the cultures and cuisines of people who inhabit a geographical area. You'll find that each state, region, territory, or area has its own individual set of attributes within any country. For example, the northwest region of the United States is home to several national forests and some of the most breathtaking natural features in the country. Cities like Portland and Seattle have some of the highest living standards in the country – yet only a couple hours away, small towns seem frozen in time – places that would have felt familiar to someone from the 1970s or 1980s.

For example, in Washington state, there's a town called Forks (population around 4000). It has one main street with a grocery store, a couple of gas stations, some restaurants and bars. There's not much nightlife. What drives the economy is their tourism sector as the town became famous due to author Stephanie Meyer's *Twilight* series.

There are many other towns like Forks, also with a population under 5000. In these small towns, people live simpler lives. They hunt and fish, ride horses and drive tractors, and enjoy views of the majestic mountains all around them. It's a region with a texture unlike anywhere else in the USA.

Then there is Florida, a state found in the south-eastern United States. It is well-known for being a peninsula and having over 1,000 miles of beaches on its coastline. The state is delighted to be home to over 21+ million people and has also provided a large amount of America's orange juice.

You may also note that within different regions (for example, South America), there are many cultures. South America is the fourth large continent globally and consists of twelve independent countries. The region's geographical Diversity is immense; it ranges from Andes Mountains in the west to Amazon Rainforest in the east, and from Chile's dry Atacama Desert in the north to Tierra del Fuego's forests and penguins' colonies in the extreme south. There are 400 million people who call this continent their home, speaking over four hundred different languages and dialects.

South America can be divided into the Andean countries, Central America and the Caribbean communities, the Southern Cone nations, and the Amazonian states. These regions have diverse geographical features and cultures. They have similarities in language, food, and lifestyle, but they also have characteristics unique to their region.

The United States of America is one of the most diverse countries globally, but each region comprises distinct populations and unique cultural and linguistic traditions. The differences between northerners and southerners have become so pronounced that they can be described as separate subcultures. There are many examples that highlight this: their food, celebrations and practices, fashion trends and even their speech patterns.

While there are some consistencies among all American states, there are substantial differences between the northern and southern states. Perhaps the best examples are in the states' southern regions. The South differs from the rest of the United States largely due to its history and culture.

The history of the South begins with Native Americans, such as the Cherokee, Choctaw, Creek,

Chickasaw, and Seminole, who lived along the coast and interior. Most were farmers and hunters who raised their families near one of the many rivers that flowed into the Atlantic. Settlers from Europe arrived in America soon after Columbus's discovery of the New World in 1492. However, the English, French and Spanish dominated colonizing and settling the North American continent. The English arrived in Virginia in 1607; settlers arrived in Jamestown (Virginia) and established the first colony and settled mainly along the east coast of America. The Spanish settled mainly in what is now Florida and California. The French settled mainly in Canada around Quebec and on the Mississippi River.

The first Europeans arrived in 1513; they sailed along the coast looking for gold. They set up colonies on the coast 13 years later. The Spanish settlers initially controlled the southern states, but the European settlers in the north eventually overtook them. This was accomplished through wars and annexations, the most significant of which was the Spanish American War. This conflict resulted in the European settlers taking control of the southern states from the Spanish.

Southern culture is often romanticized in popular media, but you might be surprised to learn how different the Southern culture is based on the region you're in. From politics to attitudes toward race and gender, there are many cultural differences between Southern states.

The culture of the southern United States is a distinct flowering of American culture. The region's population is politically conservative, patriotic, religious, and committed to traditional norms of morality. The South has become a battleground in the fight over the future of American culture, with many of the nation's most bitter political battles being fought over social issues.

But the history of the Northern States in the USA is a journey from small, sparsely populated colonies to densely populated regions. The North experienced a different history than that of the South, and many factors played into this. These included its geography, population growth, economy and involvement in various wars.

During the American Revolution and the War of 1812, New England and the mid-Atlantic states were considered the true heartland of the nation. Territories such as Virginia, North Carolina, Tennessee, and Kentucky were too remote and their populations too sparse for many cultural similarities to exist. Market interests varied between northern and southern states, prohibiting economic alliance. However, during this period, commonalities consistently emerged amongst the northern states that fostered a greater sense of community.

With the geographical makeup of states in the United States, there is no lack of Diversity. In fact, some states are completely unrecognizable compared to others, North and South Dakota for instance. The two Dakotas are strikingly different in terms of their geography and demographics. North Dakota is a largely rural and agricultural state, while South Dakota is more urban and industrialized. The population of North Dakota is predominantly White, while the population of South Dakota is more diverse, with a significant Native American population. The economy of North Dakota is based largely on agriculture and natural resources, while the economy of South Dakota is more diversified, with a stronger manufacturing sector.

Each state in the USA offers unique geography, untouched by modern civilization. These states contain large amounts of land with ecosystems that have been unchanged for thousands of years. The landscape in certain parts of the United States has the potential to be preserved like no other place in the entire world.

Throughout the years, the United States of America has been known for its numerous geographic and topographical features, allowing for multiple industries to arise in the economy. The differences in flora and fauna from state to state are among the most striking differences within the country. The wide variety of terrain found in the United States can be attributed to a number of factors, including geography, climate, and exposure to natural occurrences such as volcanic activity.

If you examined the geographical land-use picture of the world, you would be surprised to discover that countries differ in the way they use their surface. Land use or Land Cover combines natural and artificial materials on the ground that is visible with bare eyes or captured by satellite or aerial photography. The land-use decision reflects the interest and priorities of each country.

People have inhabited the earth since prehistoric times. With time, human civilizations evolved and developed distinct types of cultures and different lifestyles. All have come to existence based on different natural resources that inhabit each geographical region.

The history of humanity is rich with a beautiful array of civilizations. These societies include the Sumerian, which is believed to be the earliest civilization. Many ancient civilizations had their fair share in developing our world today.

As we all know, geography is the key factor in the formation and development of ancient cultures. Geography refers to the physical land around us and the environment's impact on human society—the natural resources available for trade or exploitation, for example. And when one civilization meets another civilization, their different geographic locations determine what kinds of cultural and commercial interactions can take place.

When people think about Ancient Civilizations, a few of the most well-known empires often pop up in their minds, such as Ancient Egypt, the Roman Empire, and the Aztec tribe. But did you know about some of the other great civilizations that existed throughout time? For example, the Sargon of Akkad, who united all of Mesopotamia under a single empire, or Machiavelli's Florence, with its innovative approach to government and economics.

The geographic location and climate in which a civilization developed yielded many advantages and disadvantages. Some ancient civilizations thrived because the ocean surrounded them, or because the climate was optimal for their crops. Other ancient civilizations did not survive long because they were in remote areas with no natural borders. This is a great example of how separation and isolation can lead to termination. For entities to thrive and survive, different ways are necessary. Geographical Diversity is more important than ever before because the more diverse our surroundings the more chances we have to interact with people from different cultures and backgrounds.

The world history of human civilization has been largely shaped by geographical constraints and the diverse civilizations that have thrived in different parts of the world. The geography of today's world is shaped by the collision of continents, erosion over millennia, severe atmospheric changes, glacial activities, and the effect of human activities on rivers and oceans. Geographical distribution has played a significant role in shaping the very history of human civilization.

Our beautiful blue planet is home to diverse cultures, languages, ethnicities, religions, and geography. Even in the same country, there might be significant differences in livelihood, standards of living, and general wealth, as seen in the differences between the northern and southern states in the USA.

We all talk about the importance of Diversity on a societal level — in our workplaces, schools, and neighborhoods — but what about a global scale? We know it's important to have a variety of nationalities working together in our communities, companies, and schools to promote an environment of harmony where all backgrounds can come together, interact with one another, and coexist.

On a global scale, we have Diversity and collaboration in the United Nations. The formation of the United Nations is one of the most important events in human history. In 1945, representatives from 50 nations signed the charter for the United Nations and created an international organisation whose stated aims were to maintain international peace and security, develop friendly relations among nations and overcome conflicts, if any, leaving behind a legacy of goodwill, peace and human rights. Diversity has been an essential part of this network because different cultures and societies have been bringing different ideas about their culture into the table for discussion; their success depends heavily on how effectively these different societies can come together.

What's more, everything is interconnected. In other words, we need each other, and our differences constitute our strength as a planet. Diversity is the foundation for progress and sustainability of our planet.

CHAPTER 5

DIVERSITY IN EMPLOYMENT

Until a few years ago, having multiple streams of income was not seen as a need. Mostly, America has had a culture of going to college and getting a degree or graduating high school and entering the workforce. No matter which path was taken, the end goal was to land a well-paying job with good benefits. Once the job was secured, the goal switched to building a career, most often with the same employer.

The economy was doing well enough that people could do this and still support themselves comfortably. However, in recent years that has changed, and many Americans live from one week to the next and falling deeper into debt with no security.

The number of people living paycheck-to-paycheck is staggering. Most Americans live from one paycheck to the next with little to no money left over for savings or emergencies. According to a study by CNBC, 62 percent of Americans live paycheck-to-paycheck, and 42 percent of those same people make more than $100,000 a year. This means that even small bumps in the road can be very difficult for many people to handle. People are finding out more each day that it's never good to "put all of your eggs in one basket." This one job gig is no longer sustainable.

For example, an unexpected medical bill or a car repair can throw an already-tight budget out of whack. It's hard enough when you're trying to deal with a financial emergency while living within your means. It's even harder when you don't have any financial wiggle room at all.

Even if a person isn't dealing with an emergency, living paycheck-to-paycheck often means that they're spending more than they would like on interest payments, late fees, and overdraft fees — just because they don't have the cash to cover unexpected expenses or upcoming bills.

The COVID-19 pandemic that shut down the world in 2020 was possibly the biggest 'financial emergency' the majority of people have ever faced in their lives. When everything came to a halt and people could not leave their homes, many were thrown into a panic because they only had one source of income.

People with savings to fall back on continued to make ends meet without worrying too much about their finances. For others, however, this was not the case, and fear set in as they pondered how they would manage without an income coming in. However, even for the people who were fortunate enough to have savings, those funds soon dried up when companies downsized or closed down for good and millions found themselves unemployed and, to some degree destitute. Another result of the pandemic was that millions of people lived at or near the poverty line, with no sign of recovery.

The average family income, as measured by the Census Bureau, was $67,521 in 2020. That's not good news, especially considering the rising cost of living. This means that one source of income, especially in these uncertain times we live in, is just not enough.

The cost of living has contributed to the rapid increase in the number of people finding it difficult to make their monthly financial obligations. However, it is not the only thing to blame for our current financial woes.

Advances in technology have made life easier, but they have also resulted in mass job losses. According to a report by McKinsey Global Institute, it is estimated that 60 percent of the American workforce will be automated by 2030. This means there is a chance that robotics and AI will replace middle-class jobs in America by 2030. Unfortunately, this also means that even highly educated professionals are at risk of losing their jobs due to technological advances.

So much has changed in a short while. First, the economy is not what it was a few decades ago. The unemployment rate, for example, has dropped from 5.7 percent in 2002 to 4.0 percent in 2022, according to the U.S. Bureau of Labor Statistics. While this seems like a positive statistic, the jobs available are not what they were in 2002, and there are fewer opportunities.

One may argue there are more positions than ever before, but they are part-time or contract positions rather than full-time jobs with benefits such as retirement accounts and health insurance. There are also increases in outsourcing which means the jobs available may be temporary or lower-paying positions that cannot offer full benefits packages or high salaries. This is because the minimum wage has not been raised in over ten years (since 2009), while the cost of living has risen exponentially over that same period of time.

Forty million Americans live below the poverty line and that number is growing every year. The poverty rate is the highest it's been in two decades, and more Americans are living in extreme poverty than ever before. A full-time worker earning the current federal minimum of $7.25 per hour makes only about $15,000 a year. That income puts a family of four at almost twice the poverty level (i.e., below what's necessary for necessities). The current federal minimum wage has not just failed to keep up with inflation; its value is 30 percent lower than it was in 1968 after adjusting for inflation. You can agree that $15,000 is not a living wage.

While this is terrible, what is even worse is that many other countries around the globe - including developed ones - don't even have a minimum wage.

This severe lack of adequate remuneration has left many seeking other options to make an extra dollar, and thus many have fully embraced gig economy. It has not only raised their standard of living, but also offers more financial security. Once again, Diversity is the only answer to a problem that seemingly was not solvable.

Let us briefly rewind to the 90s. The workforce was drastically different from what it is today. The most prominent careers included manufacturing, farming, mining, and construction jobs. There were no smartphones or tablets, only desktop computers with dial-up access to the Internet. Microsoft Office was still in its infancy, and email was just beginning to be adopted as a business communication tool.

High school graduates and college students did not have to worry about finding a job after graduation. Their only worry was which job offer they would accept. Getting a job was easy, and employees stayed at their jobs for years — sometimes even decades.

Fast forward two decades and the scene has changed dramatically. Employers now struggle to attract and retain talent as the competition for skilled workers has intensified.

In the 2000s, due to a technological revolution, the world's biggest economies were reshaped into what they are today. This has not only led to more efficient and sustainable output but also opened up new job opportunities for people who would have otherwise been left behind.

Nowadays, it's much more common to see people with several side hustles besides their regular job as they try to maximize their income and personal financial security. The need to have multiple streams of income is greater now than ever.

Enter the gig economy. The gig economy is also known by other names, including "sharing economy" and "on-demand economy." It is a labor market characterized by the prevalence of short-term contracts or freelance work as opposed to permanent jobs. Although there are many companies now that support "gigs" like Uber and Door Dash, working a second or sometimes, the third job is not a new phenomenon.

Selling real estate, for example, used to be the classic option for a side job that would allow people to build an income from multiple streams. Independent contracting is not new; it's been a part of the workforce for decades. However, it has become more common in the past few years as organizations have learned that they can save money by hiring contract workers instead of adding new full-time employees. It's also become more attractive to workers who want more flexibility.

The gig economy started during the economic recession of the late 2000s. In 2009, as unemployment rates were skyrocketing, firms were reluctant to add new permanent employees. Instead, they hired freelancers and consultants on a project basis to meet their needs without long-term obligations.

The gig economy is one of the big shifts in the Diversity of how people earn money that's occurred throughout history. In the Industrial Revolution of the 19th century, people moved from being farmers to factory workers. Nowadays, many have gone from working for a single company to making money through various jobs and freelancing.

Because of the Covid-19 pandemic, many businesses have shut down temporarily or permanently to which the gig economy became a lifeline. According to Statista Research Department, there were 57.3 million freelancers in the United States in 2021.

Below are some examples of work arrangements that encompass the gig economy:

- Freelance workers - Upwork, 99designs, Toptal, etc.

- Contracted work - Virtual assistants, bloggers, web developers, etc.

- On-demand services - TaskRabbit, Amazon Flex, AirBnB, etc.

- Ridesharing or delivery drivers - Uber, Lyft, Postmates, etc.

The number of freelancers in the US workforce is expected to grow from 57 million in 2017 to 86.5 million by 2027, replacing traditional forms of employment and becoming the dominant model for how people work, according to a new study by Statista.

It also suggests that traditional employment-for-benefits models will no longer be sustainable for businesses under pressure from digital disruption and competition. Instead, they will be forced to build their own freelance talent pools.

What this all boils down to is diversification of employment and generating income from different sources. When people hear the term "side hustle," it's natural to think of Uber drivers, Airbnb hosts and other gig-economy workers. But these aren't the only options out there. Some people have a second job completely unrelated to their full-time work, such as a real estate agent, mortgage broker, online travel agent, printed merchandise, and product testing.

The current economy is proving to be extremely volatile. Many social security experts are predicting a rise in unemployment across the country. As the economy continues to shift, we'll find a greater need to become more diverse in terms of how we bring income into our households. This means it becomes increasingly important to cultivate several income streams that can work in tandem with each other.

Our focus should be on financially diversifying income instead of trying to build a singular source of income. No matter how big a single source of income becomes, the income potential over time is limited.

For instance, if you work for a company solely dependent on the local economy, and that local economy tanks, your job could be in jeopardy. But if you created a multiple income stream from various sources, you would have stronger financial security.

A similar principle can be applied to personal income. If you are solely reliant on one source of income, such as employment or investments in a single industry sector, your financial well-being is vulnerable to economic fluctuations. But by having diverse sources of income, you spread out risk and strengthen your financial position.

Today, income is no longer one-dimensional. No one can afford to rely on just one stream of income. As discussed in Chapter Two, sustained success in work and life comes from building and leveraging multiple streams of income. With the economic, political, and global climate we are in, financial security is only guaranteed in Diversity.

CHAPTER 6

DIVERSITY IN INDUSTRY

The world comprises different industries that have built the foundation of our working economy. Banking, manufacturing, farming/agriculture, transportation, medical, and technology; all these industries are essential to helping our economy continue to grow.

The efficiency, integration, and feasibility of these industries have also established the success and prosperity. Each industrial sector plays an indispensable role in a nation's economic development and should be respected for the value it brings.

The difference between industries is what makes our world unique and distinctive. It also helps us build new ideas and ways of doing things that will benefit us today and tomorrow as we expand into new markets that require new skills/expertise.

Industry is often associated with mass production, scientific management, and assembly line work. It was not until the early 1900s that people gained insight into these work environments. It was not until this time that people also understood how industry could affect their lives in so many ways. Before industrialization took place, most people were farmers or tradespeople who worked on farms or in small businesses that did not require advanced skills or technologies to produce goods. As technology improved and more people moved away from rural areas into cities where they could find jobs, factory work became more commonplace and led to an increase in wages for workers across all fields.

The history of Diversity in industry in the United States is typically broken into four main periods:

1) the pre-industrial period, from the 1600s to 1877;

2) the industrial period from around 1877 to 1964 (highly debated timeline);

3) the post-industrial period from around 1965 to 2000; and 4) the modern era from 2001 to present.

In the 1600s, the economy of the United States was largely agrarian, or rural. Most of its inhabitants lived on farms or in small towns. The economy changed dramatically in the late 1700s with the start of the Industrial Revolution in Great Britain and the influx of large numbers of European immigrants to the colonies. American manufacturing consisted primarily of small workshops and small-scale farming operations.

The first phase of economic growth in the United States began with the industrial period. During this age, agriculture was transformed into a more productive and specialized industry, leading to an increase in farm output and a rise in agricultural employment. Meanwhile, industrial production became increasingly mechanized. America's workforce shifted from agriculture to manufacturing and transportation, with most workers earning wages rather than owning their own businesses (as they had during the pre-industrial era).

The revolution also brought new wealth, but this wealth was not spread evenly. The availability of cheap labor enabled industrialists to become powerful and wealthy. In this period, economic power shifted from agricultural elites to industrial capitalists, establishing factory systems that employed wage workers.

The Industrial Revolution was characterized by a complex interplay of changes in technology, society, medicine, culture, and economics that provided people with access to an unprecedented supply of goods and services.

The impact of the Industrial Revolution on society, both positively and negatively, was substantial. Before industrialization, most of the population resided in rural areas where subsistence farming was the norm. After industrialization, there was a large shift of population growth towards urban centers, as employment opportunities developed in manufacturing industries in cities. Sometimes, entire towns were built around factories. Besides providing more employment opportunities, factories also increased wages for workers and improved their standard of living by providing better access to housing and food.

The term "post-industrial" does not mean that manufacturing ceased to be important for the economy. It does mean, however, that the economy was no longer dominated by manufacturing and extractive industries as it was in the nineteenth century and much of the twentieth century. The expansion into new industries and markets was critical for the economy to sustain over time and is a sound example of the need for Diversity to operate as the foundation.

To understand this shift into new industrial markets, consider the share of Americans who worked in farming in 1900, which was around 40 percent. By 1950, only 16 percent of Americans worked on farms; by 2000, this figure had fallen to 2 percent and 1.4 percent by 2020. The declining importance of agriculture was a major economic development during the twentieth century, reshaping American society through changes such as urbanization, electrification, and suburbanization.

- Urbanization is when increasing proportions of a country's population live in cities rather than rural areas. America's urban population grew rapidly throughout the twentieth century.

- Electrification is the widespread use of electricity as a form of energy. During the early twentieth century, electricity became used widely in homes and businesses throughout America. For example, by 1920, most American households owned electric lights and appliances.

- Suburbanization is the development of suburbs, residential areas on the outskirts of cities. Suburbanization began during World War I with the construction of housing for factory workers who had migrated to cities to work in wartime industries.

Yes, urbanization and industrialization work to eliminate rural poverty, improve quality of life, provide better healthcare and education, and create diverse systems, regions, and industries. This was realized both in the industrial and modern eras.

The modern era of information is characterized by rapid economic change and technological innovations. Computers and the internet have dramatically changed how we communicate with each other. It has also had an enormous impact on our economy by creating new jobs and industries such as web development and data analysis. When a society allows for Diversity in how and what gets shaped, then it will be sustainable.

History has proven that no one industry can provide everything we need as humans. It would be impossible for us to have all the food we needed if we had only farming and agriculture - so we need manufacturing and transportation to get the food from where it's grown to where it's needed.

When you talk about Diversity in industry, you really must think about what each industry does. Some industries support other industries - like manufacturing supporting agriculture by providing the tools necessary to bring in a good harvest. Other industries are different - like technology supporting medicine by developing new ways to diagnose or treat disease.

Each industry is diverse in its unique way. Manufacturing, for instance, has many facets like textile, wood, metal, and other materials that can create products that support other industries.

When different industries are present in an environment, there is an opportunity for economic growth. Each industry brings its unique contribution to the economy, whether through job creation or innovation, resulting in increased prosperity for everyone.

The technology industry is one of the fastest-growing and most profitable industries in the world. It includes everything from software development to web-based services to internet engineering. There are many different tech companies, including startups, established companies, and even non-profits that provide open source software for public use. As an industry, technology has also created some of the highest-paying jobs in today's society due to its growth potential.

The automotive industry is another example of how different industries can come together to create something new and innovative. Automotive manufacturing companies produce automobiles from raw materials such as steel or aluminum, which then get assembled into finished products by other manufacturers before being sold on the open market at retail locations like car dealerships or online retailers like Amazon. Besides producing cars, these manufacturers often work closely with other suppliers like engine manufacturers, who provide them with parts needed during production processes like motors and transmissions, which help complete each vehicle's design specifications before being shipped off as final saleable units ready for consumer purchase.

The healthcare industry comprises hospitals publicly owned to those that are privately owned with some being not-for-profit organizations. There are differences in the way these entities operate, and they all have a role to play for providing different types of support to communities they find themselves in. The difference can be seen in employment opportunities, operating hours and services, and healthcare products they provide, given their location.

Other industries include:

Agriculture – Agriculture includes farming, farming equipment manufacturing, animal husbandry, dairy, fisheries, and related services. The agriculture industry is one of the biggest worldwide and has been around for centuries. It provides food for billions of people across the world and raw materials for other industries.

Mining – Mining is one of the oldest industries on Earth and includes any activity that involves digging up minerals or rocks from the ground. The mining industry provides us with coal, petroleum, and other minerals used in various ways.

Aerospace – Aerospace refers to both military aircraft and commercial aircraft. Aerospace technology is advancing rapidly, and the industry itself is booming today.

Information Technology – Information technology covers various fields such as computer software, hardware manufacturing, telecommunications, and e-commerce. It's an umbrella term that refers to all types of technology that are used to process information.

Today, the internet has diversified industry by creating a new type of economy that can exist on the web. This "Internet Economy" is a term used to describe various business models that have emerged with fast internet connections and easy access to information.

The internet has become a tool that allows companies to create better products and services. Above all else, it has allowed more people access to more information, goods, and services.

One of the most popular Internet industries is eCommerce. Ecommerce, short for "electronic commerce," is trading in products or services using computer networks, such as the internet. Ecommerce businesses range from small ventures run by individuals selling artisan goods online, to billion-dollar corporations like Amazon that sell everything you need for your home and office.

In the digital economy, companies are evolving to a new model. Rather than focusing on products and processes, they are building platforms. Platforms are a key part of the digital economy because they connect consumers with producers.

The platform business model is part of the larger shift from an industrial economy to an information economy. From the pre-industrial period to the internet in the present day, we have seen a very significant shift in industry.

In simpler times, if you wanted to increase your output, you had to add more people. But today, the increased output can be achieved by leveraging technology (or machines) and adding more information. By combining, people, technology, and information — we can achieve much greater productivity.

When we step back and look at the big picture, what it tells us is that the industrial revolution completely reshaped our economy. We were at one point in time a service economy and most of our labor force was used in agriculture. The need for Diversity allowed for the introduction and integration of new industries that resulted in a more advanced economy and society.

Industry and technological innovation have evolved considerably over the years. We've gone from the pre-industrial period to the industrial revolution to today's modern world of instant communication, electronic devices and a host of other innovations. Each new development has added to our knowledge base, enabling mankind to create even more advanced technologies and think about the next big step in industry. Some may see this as a pattern that will continue infinitely into the future, as technology advances along a linear path of improvement that can only lead us forward into a bright, ever-changing technological future.

The industrial revolution has been around for many decades, and it will continue to grow and expand. Industries are diversifying the way the world works, innovating and improving upon work conditions and new methods of business operation. Because of this expanding influence, our society will continue as technology becomes more and more integrated into daily life. There is no turning back from this forward momentum.

CHAPTER 7

DIVERSITY IN THE WORKFORCE

The importance of Diversity within the workforce is often undervalued and rarely realized. Often Diversity does exist within the workforce (the number of people who are eligible to work), but not necessarily in the workplace (the number of employees of an organization.) The challenge for organizations is how to match the Diversity in the workforce to the Diversity in the workplace. Within this context, several organizations resist the belief that their workplaces must look "different". Their current picture is what they are used to, is what they have learned to manage and "control" over time. Any significant change in the organizational composition or structure can, for them, cause more confusion and fear. That is the real story behind why organizations are less inclined to act to improve Diversity in the workplace.

In discussing workplace Diversity, there are different ways of looking at the topic. One can look at a diverse workforce as an end (for example, "an organization should strive to reflect the population in which it operates"). One can view workforce Diversity as a means to an end (for example, "an organization should strive to reflect the population in which it operates because diverse perspectives and experiences make for a stronger organization).

To move our research forward, it's important to understand the factors that drive the inequalities we see in organizations today. Inequality is driven by how power, resources and opportunities are distributed across group structures. Social Dominance Theory introduced in 1999 by Jim Sidanius and Felicia Pratto suggests that social structures seem to be supported by an implicit hierarchy of group dominance. These group-based hierarchies can be based on various categories of difference, with race, gender, and socioeconomic status serving as the most salient categories.

Group-based hierarchies influence how equitable the allocation of resources is and how the distribution of undesirable work and/or roles are assigned. For example, in modern western society, White males are viewed as more dominant than any other minority racial or gender group. Further, White males who sit atop the group-based hierarchy possess the power and authority to allocate resources based on their self-interest and assign undesired roles, such as low wage jobs or living in undesirable locations, to subordinate groups. Since Sidanius and Pratto published their original theory, further work has identified the influence gender, race, age, economic status, and other factors have on social power, status, wealth, and opportunity. Group-based hierarchies are foundational to many, and perhaps all, workplaces.

By understanding how and why these group-based hierarchies develop, evolve over time, and persist across generations despite changes in laws and norms that should eradicate them, we can begin to intentionally address them and grow a more just society for all. However, these hierarchies are often viewed as fixed and static. What's more, there is an assumption these hierarchies are natural and inevitable. Because of this belief, individuals accept group-based inequality as normal and justifiable.

Moreover, there are systems at work in organizations designed to maintain the group-based hierarchies which drive conformity and prevent differences from being acknowledged and appreciated. To understand how these group-based hierarchies developed over time, we need to look back at the United States, before World War I, which started around 1917. Prior to 1917, the workforce was almost entirely male, more specifically, White male dominated. During the onset of the war, as men went off to battle, women entered the workforce, more specifically, White women entered the workforce. I make the distinction in race to signify the impact of intersectionality on how we examine gender and race. Once World War I was over, White men regained control over the workplace and most White women were left to go back to tending to the house.

We experienced a similar story with the second world war around the early 1940s. However, this time, more women remained in the workplace than after World War

I. Introducing racial minorities in the workplace was not realized until the 1960s with passing The Civil Rights Act. If you consider the period between the end of World War II and the Civil Rights Act, nearly thirty years, then you can understand how these group-based hierarchies grew stronger. Even in 2022, there are still more White male CEOs and leaders in organizations than any other racial or gender group, despite the dramatic change in the workforce demographics over the past twenty years.

These systems, derived from group-based hierarchies, permeate every facet of the organizational structure and culture including the groups likely to become managers and leaders and the groups likely considered for administrative roles. Research overwhelmingly confirms that men are hired to fill leadership roles more often than women. Minorities, mainly African Americans and Latinx are more likely to work in lower-level administrative or service roles, than Whites. These systems are baked into multiple organizational processes, including hiring, terminating, promotions, compensation, policies and practices and support the group-based hierarchies. Taking any of these processes and linking it to the group-based hierarchies, we can conclude that the group that sits at the top of the hierarchy, has the greatest advantage over all other groups.

Again, research overwhelmingly supports the realization that White men, on average, receive better compensation, fulfil more leadership roles, are hired the most but terminated the least, and are most supported by policies and practices. If this seems one-sided to you, it is, and that's the problem. I invite you to also consider that White men are primarily setting the compensation structures, hiring the leaders, deciding who gets terminated, and shaping the policies and practices. Figure 1 is a 2018 table based on a report published in the New York Times and a local North Carolina newspaper depicting the racial and gender demographics for Fortune 500 CEOs.

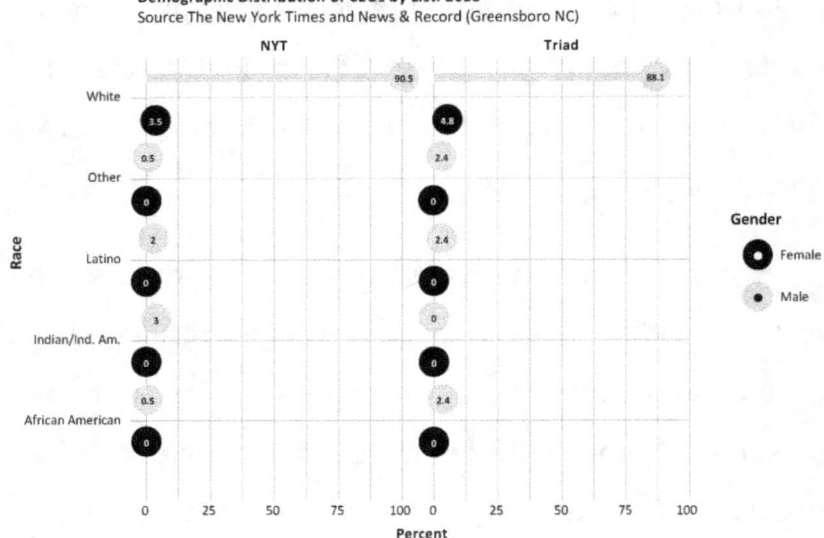

Demographic Distribution of CEOs by List. 2018
Source The New York Times and News & Record (Greensboro NC)

Figure 1

Two sources with the same outcome, White men overwhelmingly occupy leadership positions more than any other race or gender combined 4x over. As we've been describing in this book, Diversity has been the foundational component of everything that we experience in the world, our workplaces should be no different. Unfortunately, the origination of the workplace as we know it today, did not begin with Diversity of individuals as the foundation. Therefore, one solution would be to integrate Diversity to rebuild the foundation.

It's important to recognize that the reality of rebuilding the foundation of our existing workplace is and has been a slow process met with great resistance simply due to the current organizational systems designed to support the group-based hierarchies. To address slow and stagnant progress in diversifying our organizations, we can apply theoretical principles researched over time.

In 1968, a biologist named Ludwig Von Bertalanffy, developed General System Theory, which focused on understanding organizations as a system that transforms inputs into outputs through various processes or throughputs. General System Theory has been widely applied to organizations in determining the root cause of performance issues. These performance issues could include anything from slow product manufacturing time to inadequate or low sales numbers, to even poor customer service ratings. Inputs are materials, resources (human), or assignments, which cause people or processes to perform to produce outputs. Outputs are the products or outcomes produced by the people within the organization reshaping the inputs through workflows and processes. Figure 2 shows a very simplified version of General System Theory.

Essentially, if you examine a set of inputs within a system and how the processes shape the inputs into outputs, you can reasonably conclude that changing the inputs to a system, will invariably affect the outputs. If we are seeking to change the outputs of the existing organizational systems that have long supported the group-based hierarchies and to rebuild the foundation of our workplaces using Diversity as the base, then the primary focus should be on changing the inputs to the current organizational systems.

Ludwig Von Bertalanffy's
General System Theory

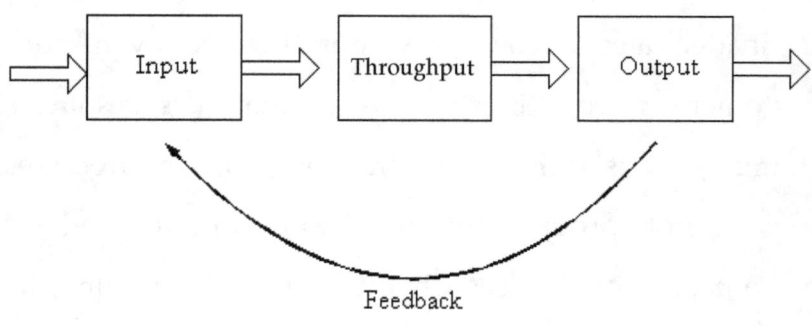

Figure 2

If organizations center Diversity, by making it a critical piece of the inputs to the organizational systems discussed earlier (hiring, terminations, compensation, promotion), then the throughputs and outputs would also be centered in Diversity. How is this done in practice? Well, some organizations have begun the work. Let's take the compensation system within an organization, for example. Centering Diversity as an input for the compensation system would look like requiring salaries within an organization to be equitable to employees of different races and genders. This can be accomplished first by conducting a pay equity study to determine if there are any disproportionate outcomes in compensation. Are the salaries for White women at ABC Company on average higher than the salaries of Latinx women for performing the same job?

Data is a powerful tool that can lead to action. Collecting demographic data on hiring, terminations, compensation, and promotions is another input centered in Diversity and can affect the output. Most organizations do not collect this type of data but should regularly.

Collecting and tracking the data is good, but not enough. Once the data is examined and disparities are found, the organization must correct those disparities. Here is where most organizations experience resistance and can fall back into operating within the group-based hierarchies. Correcting a disparity such as one related to equitable compensation, will mean that some employees (most likely those most underrepresented) will receive what may appear to be a huge bump in pay and others will not. Using our previous example, to correct the pay disparity may mean that ABC Company will increase the salaries of only the Latinx women employees to be on par with that of the White women employees. This also means that the White women employees will not receive a pay increase, which may appear unfair to those employees. However, the pay was inequitable the entire time and the organization is simply correcting the mistake.

The impact of group-based hierarchies is stronger when there is little Diversity within the group of decision-makers. It's easier to justify not implementing an action that will address the inequities of a smaller group, when a norm of the group-based hierarchy is that the higher a group is on the hierarchy, the more power granted to that group. This is an implicit and at times, explicit norm associated with group-based hierarchies. If we seek to center Diversity by breaking down the organizational reliance on group-based hierarchies, we might examine different system inputs that change the demographics of leadership within an organization.

The extent to which the demographics of leadership should change is not a hard and fast percentage. However, there are existing theories we can point to, to address this issue. There is the theory of critical mass that suggest that at least 30 percent of a minority group present in an environment is needed to have any impact on change. If critical mass theory is applied as an input, then the organization would have to change the leadership demographics to represent at least 30 percent minorities.

While I don't feel that critical mass theory is ideal, it can be a start and certainly centers Diversity as an input. An ideal representation would be one where there is no majority of one group present in the leadership. It may seem like a utopia, but we are not that far off as the U.S. Census projects that on or about 2060, there will be no majority group. Of course, 2060 is nearly 40 years into the future, but if organizations center Diversity in the inputs to the hiring and promotion systems, then the outputs will disrupt the reliance on the group-based hierarchies.

Once an organization begins to breakdown the group-based hierarchies through centering Diversity by way of changing the inputs to the organizational systems of hiring, terminations, promotions, compensation, the DRIVE Principle referred to in Chapter 1 can be fully realized. Diversity allows organizations to Reveal a demonstration of strong Initiative, to realize a true Vision of current state and future state and to meet and possibly exceed Expectations.

CHAPTER 8

DIVERSITY AS THE FOUNDATION FOR EQUITY AND INCLUSION

It is often stated that in America, anyone can accomplish anything they want as long as they work hard. This notion gives way to the deeply rooted belief that everyone has a chance to be successful. However, if we consider where this thinking originated and who it was actually meant for, we can see how this notion is not applicable to "anyone". Despite the obvious counternarratives of the lived experiences of people not of the dominant group (for whom that quote was meant), the belief is still engrained in American society.

Structural systems in America that allow for individual prosperity were originally designed for and by one group, Whites. These systems include education, financial, judicial/legal, health, housing, etc. As American society included more diverse groups, the dominant group still remained in power. The systems were still structured to support the needs of that group. It is ludicrous to believe that the systems designed centuries ago to support one group, can somehow be automatically applied to other groups. The obvious remedy is to reshape these systems so they no longer favor just one group, but that they support many groups.

This narrative shows the power of Diversity. The more Diversity is cultivated, the greater the chance that society can be reshaped to address historical exclusions and inequities and, therefore, lead to more inclusivity. Diversity is necessary for equity and inclusion to work.

To embrace the need for Diversity, individuals must first come to terms with their own personal biases -this is what we call achieving self-awareness. It can be a challenging experience to unlearn behaviors applied for years based on false beliefs about people from different groups. What makes it even more difficult is the constant perpetuation of these false beliefs through vicarious learning mediums, such as (social and live media, and television).

The path to self-awareness can begin by personally interacting with people whose group identities differ from our own. Through these individual experiences, we may develop an awareness that defies the false beliefs we previously held. Further, one must examine and acknowledge the differences between how a person from the dominant group navigates society vs. a person from a non-dominant group. What privileges are inherently afforded to the dominant group, the group that sits atop the group-based hierarchies in organizations?

Research from Harvard sociologist Devah Pager in 2004 revealed that White applicants who are ex-felons are more likely to receive callbacks for a job interview than Black applicants with no criminal record. Another example is the 2020 report issued by Georgetown University's Center on Education in the Workforce. The report titled "The Unequal Race for Good Jobs" concluded that White workers with a bachelor's degree overwhelmingly land more of the "good jobs" relative to their Black and Hispanic counterparts with similar education. Figure 3 shows the actual results of the report and it's evident how much of a gap exists between White workers and everyone else.

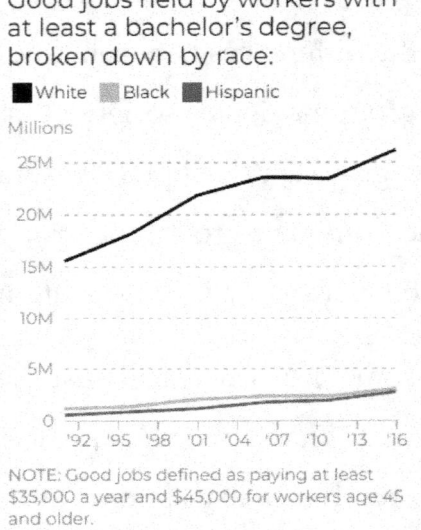

Who's got the good jobs?

Good jobs held by workers with at least a bachelor's degree, broken down by race:

■ White ■ Black ■ Hispanic

NOTE: Good jobs defined as paying at least $35,000 a year and $45,000 for workers age 45 and older.
SOURCE: Georgetown University Center on Education and the Workforce; U.S. Census Bureau

Mitchell Schnurman/DMN

Figure 3

These and other research studies confirm the privilege of getting selected for a job simply due to your placement on the group-based hierarchy. The other side of that coin is the marginalization and exclusion that happens with other groups who do not inherently have privilege. The stereotypes associated with racial groups often shape how they are perceived by others in the workplace. For instance, Black women report experiencing micro-aggressions daily at work — things like being mistaken for a peer's assistant, feeling like their voices go unheard during meetings, and that their ideas are dismissed as "too radical" or "too aggressive." Imagine having to go to work every day and multiple times a day having to prove to others that you are not how society has labelled you. Every day, this is a constant battle for people of color.

Diversity refers to the representation of difference, or percentage of difference in a population. It can be measured in terms of race, gender, age, sexual orientation, religion, and ability, and other identity factors. Inclusion is a qualitative measure that examines how the differences in individuals contribute to our population. For example, do employees feel that their differences are valued and, therefore, they feel included, supported, and empowered by the organization? Or do employees feel like they have to assimilate into or adhere to the group-based hierarchies that exist. Equity is about the measures required to change the imbalance of access and opportunity.

Many companies and industries struggle with broadening the composition of their workforce to create a unique blend of Diversity. Most organizations are stuck in homogeneity as the model for an employee population because that has been the case since their inception. To envision a workplace that is a representation of the world requires a disruption of the mindset that the model workplace is mostly made of White employees, with White men holding most, if not all of the leadership positions. And if there are Black, Latinx, Asian, Native American or other non-White employees, they would work in the lower wage areas of the organization. It's easy to examine this practice and realize that the roots of slavery in the US and across the world, still permeate our society today.

Diversity seeks to expand and improve societal environments through the rich representation of people from different backgrounds, cultures, identities, walks of life, etc. Just as the world is shaped with difference as we've discussed in previous chapters, our society and workplaces should be also. When Diversity is the foundation, we can create spaces that allow for the full expression and integration of multiple ways of being in the world.

Equity is not just about fairness; it's about social justice and the provision of access to basic needs for all groups to contribute to society. Equity recognizes there are historic and contemporary barriers that prevent equitable access and opportunities for groups of people historically oppressed through laws and social structures and therefore, made to feel and treated as less than the dominant group. These groups are often called marginalized. Every term used in the Diversity, equity and inclusion philosophy has a distinct meaning. Due to historical laws and structures designed by and for the dominant group, a redistribution of resources must effectively address the imbalance of access that exists. Part of changing the inputs to the organizational systems discussed in Chapter 7, requires equity, but must first be centered in Diversity for equity to work.

For example, if we examine the degree of poverty that individuals in low-income areas experience relative to other, more affluent areas, we have to ask ourselves, why there is such a huge disparity within these two communities. What resources have been provisioned to the people in affluent areas that the people in low-income areas have not received? This requires us to look beneath the surface and when we do so, we'll begin to see associations with people who live in low-income areas with poorer health, shorter lifespans, unhealthier living conditions, than people who live in affluent communities. Again, as we examine this deeper, we'll see this outcome is by design. As mentioned, historically, laws and social structures that we still live under today, were designed by and for the dominant group that sits atop the group-based hierarchies. Other groups historically marginalized, cannot reap the benefits of these social structures. Therefore, the structures must change in order for the marginalized groups to have access and opportunity to the resources these structures provide to thrive in society.

Imagine a society where there is no low-income housing, but rather affordable housing for everyone. Imagine a nation where your zip code does not determine your life expectancy. Imagine a world, where the race you were born into does not predetermine how you navigate through society. Imagine a world where your gender identity does not determine the employment or career you can have or the pay you can receive for performing that job. We have reached a time in our world where social change is necessary. As we look at the changing demographics around race, age, and gender identity, the need to center Diversity has never been greater. It can no longer be acceptable to adhere to or perpetuate the group-based hierarchies that exist in our organizations or our society.

The world witnessed a day of great transparency when George Floyd, a Black man, was murdered by a police officer in Minneapolis, Minnesota in the summer of 2020 and it was all caught on video. This marked a period of social justice protests across the world. Millions of people from all over the world demonstrated their solidarity with the Black communities in the United States. In reaction to this worldwide protest, many companies decided to issue solidarity statements and announce several commitments to "do better." This experience was coupled with a worldwide pandemic (Covid-19), which blew the covers off of the health disparities that have always existed across the world, where once again, the Black community had experienced the highest mortality rates. Perhaps the summer of 2020 marked a turning point in our nation to acknowledge the historical systemic oppression that people of color have experienced for centuries. Several companies have made a number of commitments to racial equity without changing the lives of people of color or without changing the demographics of their leadership structure. The group-based hierarchy is still at play.

Organizations are still struggling with how to change, why they should change, and what will happen if we do change. Part of progress is resistance, especially when changing requires you not be in the driver's seat or not have as much power and authority or recognizing that the privilege that your life has been built around will be compromised. Many leaders in organizations face a decision to maintain or break down the group-based hierarchies that exist. It's an easy decision to maintain the group-based hierarchies or continue to justify their placement in the organizations through notions of the lack of diverse talent available or "we've always done it this way," or "if we change too much too fast or we'll lose everyone."

While companies should be held accountable for their promises of support and solidarity, they are not. Many companies simply wait until their previous statement expires, then issue a new statement suggesting they still care about racial justice. But they do not actively support racial justice by improving working conditions for Black and Latinx employees — especially those who work in low-wage jobs in retail stores and restaurants. For example, major retailers often serve as hiring centers for immigrant workers, many of whom are undocumented and vulnerable to exploitation through wage theft and other forms of discrimination.

Whether or not these companies' commitments to racial equity are genuine, is not the issue. The problem is that most are failing to acknowledge and then disrupt the systems of oppression within themselves, which allow them to continue benefiting from those systems. It is a constant wrestle with whether to maintain the group-based hierarchies. Meaningful Diversity and group-based hierarchies cannot coexist in an environment. One will always cancel out the other. In order for Diversity to be centered, the group-based hierarchies must be dismantled.

This is obviously not an easy task when you reflect on the fact that even though the institution of slavery in the United States was abolished in 1865, over one hundred and fifty-five years ago, we are still experiencing "firsts". For example, in 2022, the first Black woman, was appointed to the U.S. Supreme Court. However, there is still hope and many people believe that eventually, the systems of oppression and the group-based hierarchies will be broken down and a new structure will be created that will respect, acknowledge, and afford power to all people. The most important factor that will shape that belief into reality is the centering of Diversity.

REFERENCES

"15 Surprising Workplace Diversity Statistics (2022) | Apollo Technical". *Apollo Technical LLC*, 2021, https://www.apollotechnical.com/workplace-Diversity-statistics/.

"A Brief History Of Education In The United States". *Saylordotorg.Github.Io*, https://saylordotorg.github.io/text_sociology-understanding-and-changing-the-social-world-comprehensive-edition/s19-01-a-brief-history-of-education-i.html.

"A Brief History Of The Stock Market". *Sofi*, 2021, https://www.sofi.com/learn/content/history-of-the-stock-market

Adhikari, Saugat et al. "The 10 Oldest Ancient Civilizations That Have Ever Existed". *Ancient History Lists*, 2021.

"Aerospace Industry Spotlight | Selectusa.Gov". *Selectusa.Gov*, https://www.selectusa.gov/aerospace-industry-united-states.

"Ag And Food Sectors And The Economy". *Economic Research Service U.S. DEPARTMENT OF AGRICULTURE*, 2022, https://www.ers.usda.gov/data-products/ag-and-food-statistics-charting-the-essentials/ag-and-food-sectors-and-the-economy/.

Amadeo, Kimberly. "How The 2008 Lehman Brothers Collapse Affects You Today". *The Balance*, 2021, https://www.thebalance.com/lehman-brothers-collapse-causes-impact-4842338.

"Andrew Carnegie". *HISTORY*, 2021, https://www.history.com/topics/19th-century/andrew-carnegie#section_3.

Beattie, Andrew. "The Birth Of Stock Exchanges". *Investopedia*, 2021, https://www.investopedia.com/articles/07/stock-exchange-history.asp.

Bloomenthal, A. (2022). *Can a Family Survive on the US Minimum Wage?* Investopedia. Retrieved 4 March 2022, from https://www.investopedia.com/articles/personal-finance/022615/can-family-survive-us-minimum-wage.asp.

Bonvillian, William B. "US Manufacturing Decline And The Rise Of New Production Innovation Paradigms - OECD". *Oecd.Org*, https://www.oecd.org/unitedstates/us-manufacturing-decline-and-the-rise-of-new-production-innovation-paradigms.htm.

Briney, Amanda. "Why The USA Is One Of The Most Influential Nations In The World". *Thoughtco*, 2019.

Britannica, The Editors. "Andrew Carnegie | Biography, Company, Steel, Philanthropy, Books, & Facts". *Encyclopedia Britannica*, 2021, https://www.britannica.com/biography/Andrew-Carnegie.

Bryant, Jessica. "How Many Colleges Are In The U.S.?". *Bestcolleges.Com*, 2021, https://www.bestcolleges.com/blog/how-many-colleges-in-us/.

Cairns, Hilary. "The History Of How Hbcus Began - College Raptor". *College Raptor Blog*, 2021, https://www.collegeraptor.com/find-colleges/articles/college-search/the-history-of-historically-black-colleges-and-universities-hbcus/.

"Charge Statistics (Charges Filed With EEOC) FY 1997 Through FY 2021 | U.S. Equal Employment Opportunity Commission". *Eeoc.Gov*, https://www.eeoc.gov/statistics/charge-statistics-charges-filed-eeoc-fy-1997-through-fy-2021.

City Government | City of Forks. Forkswashington.org. Retrieved 5 February 2022, from https://forkswashington.org/city-government/.

Civilian unemployment rate. U.S. Bureau of Labor Statistics. (2022). Retrieved 1 March 2022, from https://www.bls.gov/charts/employment-situation/civilian-unemployment-rate.htm.

Davies, Simon. "Describe The Theory Of Change". *Betterevaluation*, 2021, https://www.betterevaluation.org/en/managers_guide/step_2/describe_theory_of_change.

Delgado, R. (1989). Storytelling for Oppositionists and Others: A Plea for Narrative. Michigan Law Review, 87(8), 2411-2441

Dickler, J. (2022). *Despite rising wages, 61% of Americans are still living paycheck to paycheck, report finds*. CNBC. Retrieved 4 March 2022, from https://www.cnbc.com/2022/02/17/wages-are-rising-but-many-americans-still-live-paycheck-to-paycheck.html

"Diversity Wins: How Inclusion Matters". *Mckinsey & Company*, 2021, https://www.mckinsey.com/featured-insights/Diversity-and-inclusion/Diversity-wins-how-inclusion-matters.

Duca, John V. "Subprime Mortgage Crisis | Federal Reserve History". *Federalreservehistory.Org*, 2013, https://www.federalreservehistory.org/essays/subprime-mortgage-crisis.

Elsesser, Kim. "Goldman Sachs Won't Take Companies Public If They Have All-Male Corporate Boards". *Forbes*, 2020,

"Employee Stock Ownership Plan (ESOP)". *Corporate Finance Institute*, 2021, https://corporatefinanceinstitute.com/resources/careers/compensation/employee-stock-ownership-plan-esop/.

Eswaran, Vijay. "The Business Case For Diversity Is Now Overwhelming. Here's Why". *World Economic Forum*, 2019, https://www.weforum.org/agenda/2019/04/business-case-for-Diversity-in-the-workplace/.

"European Colonization of North America." Nationalgeographic.org. Retrieved 2 February 2022, from https://www.nationalgeographic.org/topics/european-colonization-north-america/?q=&page=1&per_page=25.

European Colonization of the Americas. (2020, December 26). *New World Encyclopedia*. Retrieved 20:36, February 2, 2022 from https://www.newworldencyclopedia.org/p/index.php?title=European_Colonization_of_the_Americas&oldid=1047104.

Forks, Washington Facts for Kids. Kids.kiddle.co. (2022). Retrieved 5 February 2022, from https://kids.kiddle.co/Forks,_Washington.

Fotos, M., & Hebl, M. R. (2012). Organizational Diversity climate and procedural fairness: The role of Diversity centrality. Journal of Applied Psychology, 97(6), 1059-1072.

"Founded On A Set Of Beliefs - Creating The United States | Exhibitions - Library Of Congress". *Loc.Gov*, https://www.loc.gov/exhibits/creating-the-united-states/founded-on-a-set-of-beliefs.html.

Ganti, Akhilesh. "Venture Capitalist (VC)". *Investopedia*, 2021, https://www.investopedia.com/terms/v/venturecapitalist.asp.

Gig Economy Workers and Employment Benefits. Hg.org. Retrieved 1 March 2022, from https://www.hg.org/legal-articles/gig-economy-workers-and-employment-benefits-52193.

Gig economy: Number of freelancers in the U.S. 2017-2028 | *Statista.* Statista. (2022). Retrieved 4 March 2022, from https://www.statista.com/statistics/921593/gig-economy-number-of-freelancers-us/.

Goh, Frances. "10 Companies That Failed To Innovate, Resulting In Business Failure | Collective Campus". *Collectivecampus.Io,* https://www.collectivecampus.io/blog/10-companies-that-were-too-slow-to-respond-to-change#.

Google Diversity report (2014). Retrieved from Diversity.google: https://Diversity.google/reports/2014/tech-industry/

Greene, Peter. "These Five Issues Are At The Heart Of All K-12 Education Policy Debates". *Forbes,* 2020, https://www.forbes.com/sites/petergreene/2020/12/09/these-five-issues-are-at-the-heart-of-all-k-12-education-policy-debates/?sh=5d65502460d8.

Harper, David R. "Getting To Know The Stock Exchanges". *Investopedia,* 2021, https://www.investopedia.com/articles/basics/04/092404.asp.

Hernandez, Richard. "The Fall Of Employment In The Manufacturing Sector". *U.S. Bureau Of Labor Statistics,* 2018, https://www.bls.gov/opub/mlr/2018/beyond-bls/the-fall-of-employment-in-the-manufacturing-sector.htm.

Hersh, Erica. "Why Diversity Matters: Women On Boards Of Directors". *Executive And Continuing Professional Education*, 2016, https://www.hsph.harvard.edu/ecpe/why-Diversity-matters-women-on-boards-of-directors/.

Hsu, H. (2017). The Year in "Diversity Fatigue". Retrieved 11 December 2021, from https://www.newyorker.com/culture/2017-in-review/the-year-in-Diversity-fatigue

Http://www.aihec.org/who-we-serve/TCUmap.cfm

Illuzzi, K., & Tang, P. (2021). *Gig Economy Trends and Impact on Small and Medium Practices*. IFAC. Retrieved 1 March 2022, from https://www.ifac.org/knowledge-gateway/contributing-global-economy/discussion/gig-economy-trends-and-impact-small-and-medium-practices.

"Industrial Revolution". *HISTORY*, 2019, https://www.history.com/topics/industrial-revolution/industrial-revolution.

Jobs lost, jobs gained: What the future of work will mean for jobs, skills, and wages. McKinsey Global Institute. (2017). Retrieved 1 March 2022, from https://www.mckinsey.com/featured-insights/future-of-work/jobs-lost-jobs-gained-what-the-future-of-work-will-mean-for-jobs-skills-and-wages.

Krueger, Anne. "America's Muddled Industrial Policy | By Anne O. Krueger - Project Syndicate". *Project Syndicate*, 2021, https://www.project-syndicate.org/commentary/us-innovation-competition-act-misguided-industrial-policy-by-anne-o-krueger-2021-06.

Link, Arthur S. "United States | History, Map, Flag, & Population". *Encyclopedia Britannica*, 2022, https://www.britannica.com/place/United-States.

Lioudis, Nic. "The Collapse Of Lehman Brothers: A Case Study". *Investopedia*, 2021, https://www.investopedia.com/articles/economics/09/lehman-brothers-collapse.asp.

Lisa, Andrew. "History Of The American Education System". *Stacker*, 2020, https://stacker.com/stories/5541/history-american-education-system.

Mansfield, Harvey. "Niccolo Machiavelli | Beliefs, Books, The Prince, Philosophy, Accomplishments, & Facts". *Encyclopedia Britannica*, 2021.

Mark, Joshua J. "Sargon Of Akkad". *World History Encyclopedia*, 2009, https://www.worldhistory.org/Sargon_of_Akkad/.

Minimum Wage. U.S. DEPARTMENT OF LABOR. Retrieved 4 March 2022, from https://www.dol.gov/general/topic/wages/minimumwage

"Money - Gktoday". *Gktoday.In*, 2015, https://www.gktoday.in/topic/money/.

Moody, Josh. "A Guide To The Changing Number Of U.S. Universities". *US News*, 2021.

National Poverty in America Awareness Month: January 2022. Census.gov. Retrieved 4 March 2022, from https://www.census.gov/newsroom/stories/poverty-awareness-month.html.

Office of Outreach, Diversity, and Equal Opportunity: USDA ARS. (2021). Retrieved 11 December 2021, from https://www.ars.usda.gov/office-of-outreach-Diversity-and-equal-opportunity/

Pauls, Elizabeth Prine. "Native American | History, Art, Culture, & Facts". *Encyclopedia Britannica*, 2021, https://www.britannica.com/topic/Native-American.

Polatnick, M. Rivka. "Diversity in Women's Liberation Ideology: How a Black and a White Group of the 1960s Viewed Motherhood." *Signs*, vol. 21, no. 3, University of Chicago Press, 1996, pp. 679–706, http://www.jstor.org/stable/3175175.

Rosenblat, A. (2020). *Gig Workers Are Here to Stay. It's Time to Give Them Benefits.*. Harvard Business Review. Retrieved 1 March 2022, from https://hbr.org/2020/07/gig-workers-are-here-to-stay-its-time-to-give-them-benefits.

Royse, Dave. "This Day In Market History: Lehman Brothers Collapses". *Finance.Yahoo.Com*, 2019, https://finance.yahoo.com/news/day-market-history-lehman-brothers-192808024.html.

Rutherford, Max. "Diversity & Inclusion's Theory Of Change (Toc) - Diversity Professional". *Diversity Professional*, https://Diversityprofessional.com/Diversity-inclusions-theory-of-change-toc/.

Shrider, E., Kollar, M., Chen, F., & Semega, J. (2021). *Income and Poverty in the United States: 2020*. Census.gov. Retrieved 1 March 2022, from https://www.census.gov/library/publications/2021/demo/p60-273.html.

Social Dominance Theory: Definition and Examples, Study.com, https://study.com/academy/lesson/social-dominance-theory-definition-examples.html

"South America: Human Geography". *National Geographic Society*, https://www.nationalgeographic.org/encyclopedia/south-america-human-geography/.

Stahl, Ashley. "What's To Come In 2021 For Diversity, Equity And Inclusion In The Workplace". *Forbes*, 2021, https://www.forbes.com/sites/ashleystahl/2021/04/14/whats-to-come-in-2021-for-Diversity-equity-and-inclusion-in-the-workplace/?sh=2f8483857f26.

"Stock Market". *Corporate Finance Institute*, 2021, https://corporatefinanceinstitute.com/resources/knowledge/trading-investing/stock-market/.

"The Evolution Of American Agriculture — Jayson Lusk". *Jayson Lusk*, 2016, https://jaysonlusk.com/blog/2016/6/26/the-evolution-of-american-agriculture.

"The 4 Industrial Revolutions". *Institute Of Entrepreneurship Development*, 2019, https://ied.eu/project-updates/the-4-industrial-revolutions/.

The Highest Paid CEOs: Still White, Still Male - The Society Pages Richard L. Zweigenhaft, August 1, 2019, https://thesocietypages.org/specials/the-highest-paid-ceos-still-white-still-male/

The Pros and Cons of the Gig Economy. Western Governors University. (2018). Retrieved 1 March 2022, from https://www.wgu.edu/blog/pros-and-cons-gig-economy1808.html#close.

"The Top 5 Biggest U.S. Government Contracts". *Towerfast.Com*, https://www.towerfast.com/press-room/the-top-5-biggest-us-government-contracts.

Tirosh, Ofer. "Languages Of South America: The Most Spoken And Indigenous South American Languages". *Tomedes.Com*, 2021, https://www.tomedes.com/translator-hub/languages-south-america.

Topic: Gig economy in the U.S. Statista. (2021). Retrieved 1 March 2022, from https://www.statista.com/topics/4891/gig-economy-in-the-us/#dossierKeyfigures.

"TU Fast Facts". *The University Of Tulsa*, 2022, https://utulsa.edu/about/tu-fast-facts/.

Von Bertalanffy, L. (1968). *General system theory: Foundations, development,*
applications. New York: George Braziller.

Wallace, William M. "American Revolution - Prelude To War". *Encyclopedia Britannica*, 2021, https://www.britannica.com/event/American-Revolution/Prelude-to-war.

Walters, Sam. "7 Groundbreaking Ancient Civilizations That Influence Us Today". *Discover Magazine*, 2021, https://www.discovermagazine.com/planet-earth/7-groundbreaking-ancient-civilizations-that-influence-us-today.

"What Is The Weather, Climate And Geography Like In United States Of America". *World Travel Guide*, https://www.worldtravelguide.net/guides/north-america/united-states-of-america/weather-climate-geography/.

Wickham, DeWayne. "Wickham: Do You Know When Slavery Began And Ended". *Usatoday.Com*, 2014.

"Women In The Workplace 2021". *Mckinsey & Company*, 2021, https://www.mckinsey.com/featured-insights/Diversity-and-inclusion/women-in-the-workplace.

Zgola, M. (2021). *Council Post: Will The Gig Economy Become The New Working-Class Norm?* Forbes. Retrieved 1 March 2022.